The Henry Mancini
Easy Piano Collection

Photo appears courtesy of the Henry Mancini estate.

ISBN 978-1-61774-052-7

HAL•LEONARD®
CORPORATION
7777 W. BLUEMOUND RD. P.O. BOX 13819 MILWAUKEE, WI 53213

Visit Hal Leonard Online at
www.halleonard.com

ANYWHERE THE HEART GOES

from THE THORN BIRDS

Music by HENRY MANCINI
Words by WILL JENNINGS

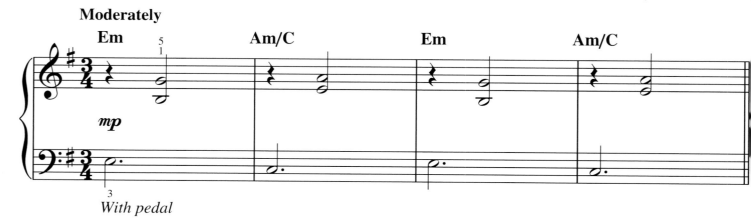

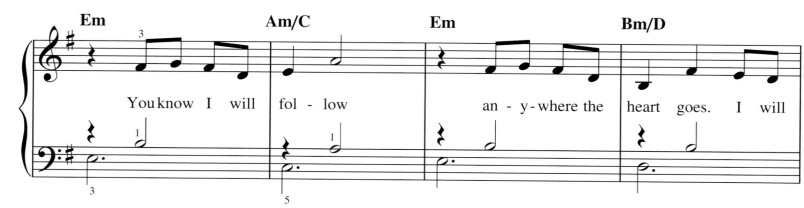

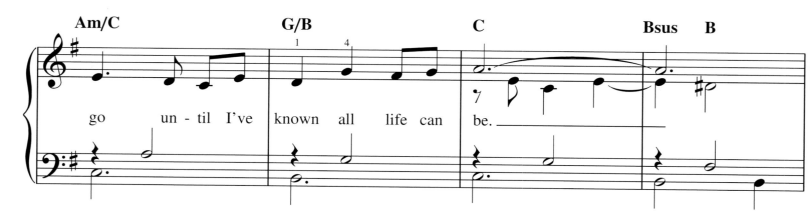

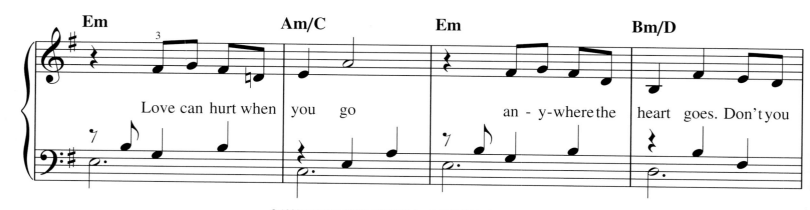

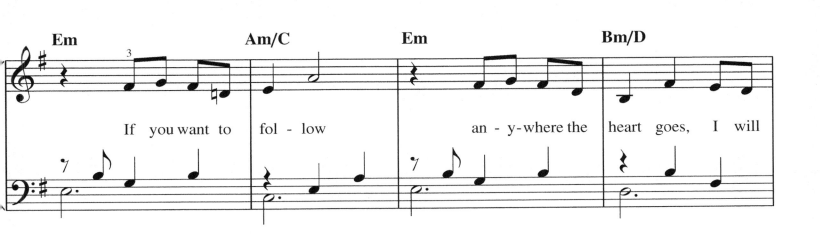

4

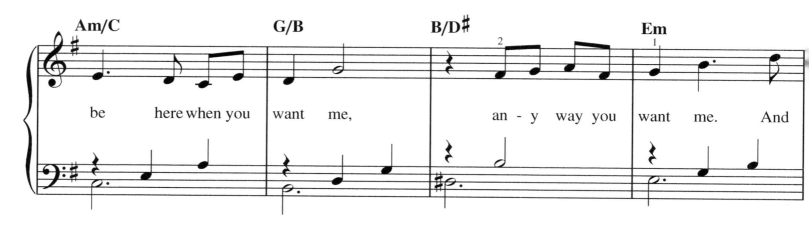

be   here when you   want   me,   an - y   way you   want   me.   And

good   years,   bad   years would   all   fall   a -   way   if   I

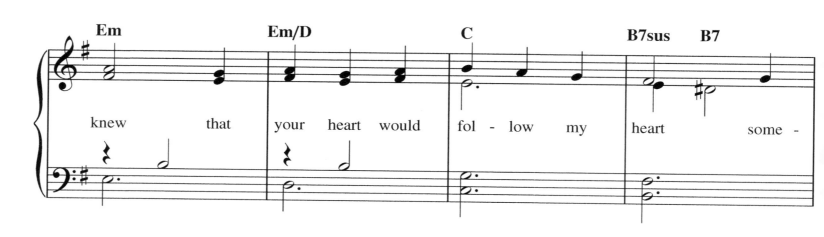

knew   that   your   heart would   fol - low   my   heart   some -

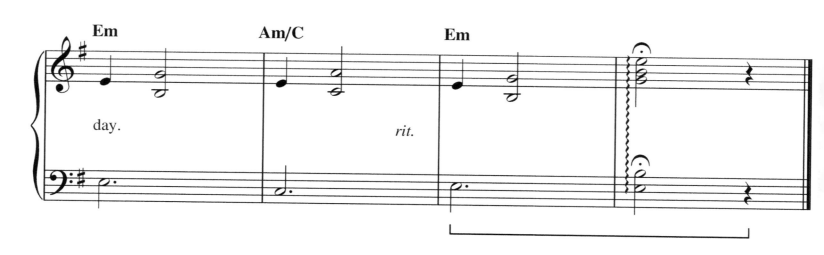

day.   *rit.*

BABY ELEPHANT WALK
from the Paramount Picture HATARI!

Words by HAL DAVID
Music by HENRY MANCINI

CHARADE
from CHARADE

Music by HENRY MANCINI
Words by JOHNNY MERCER

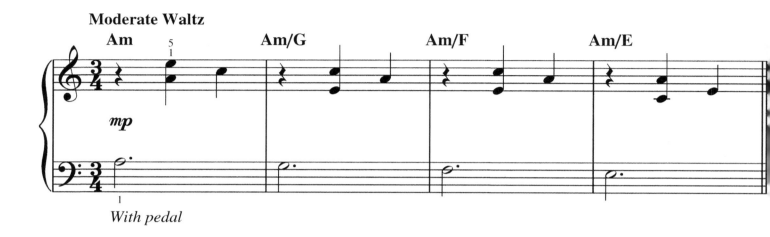

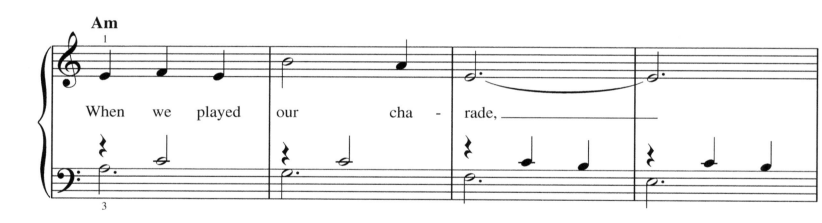

When we played our cha - rade,

we were like chil - dren pos - ing,

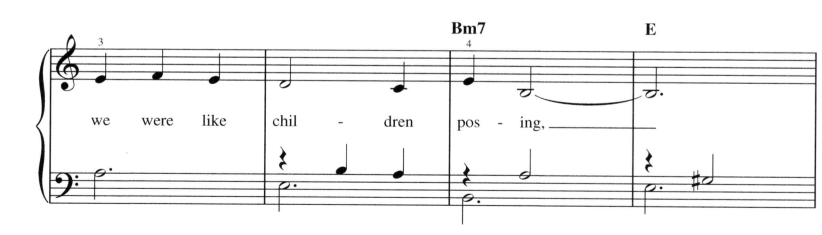

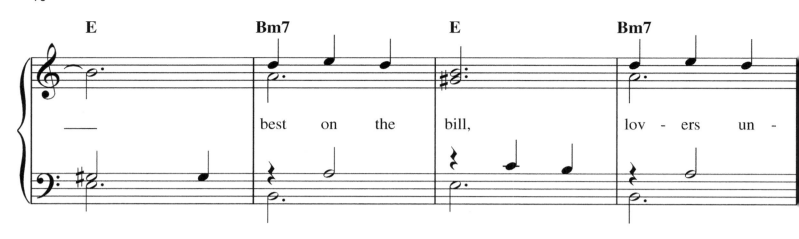

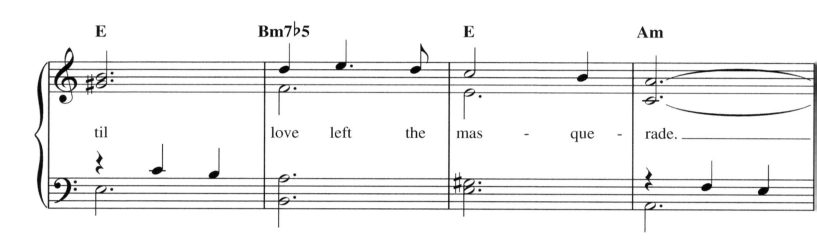

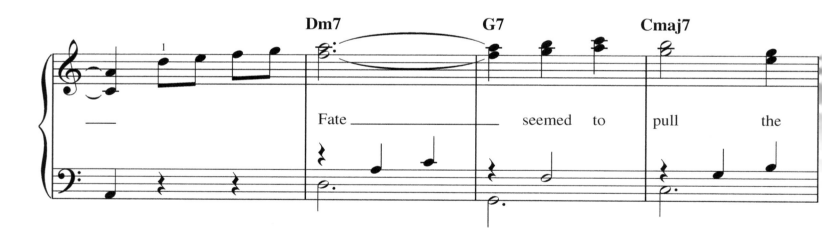

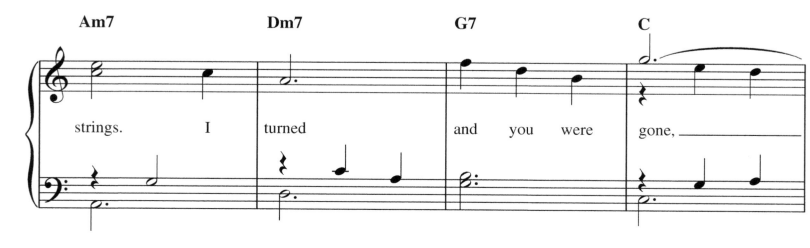

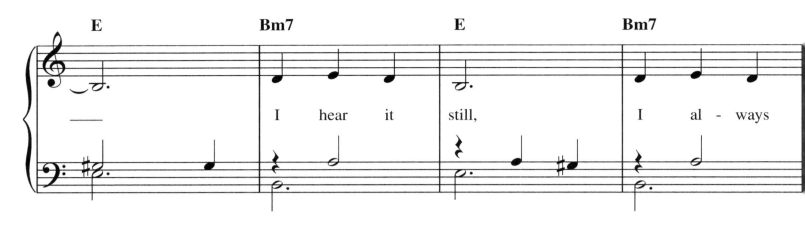

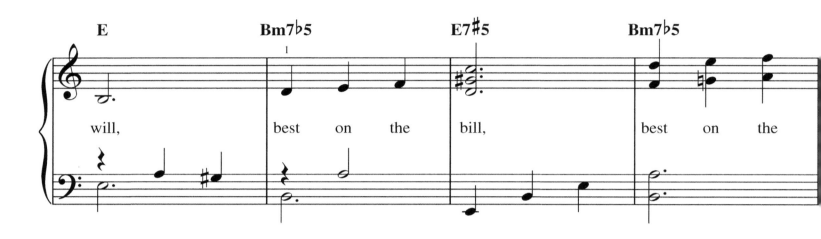

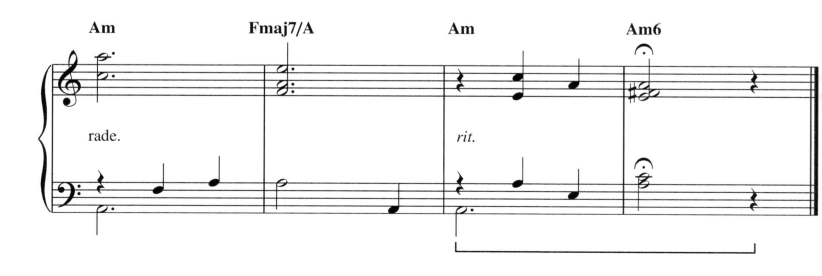

DAYS OF WINE AND ROSES

from DAYS OF WINE AND ROSES

Lyric by JOHNNY MERCER
Music by HENRY MANCINI

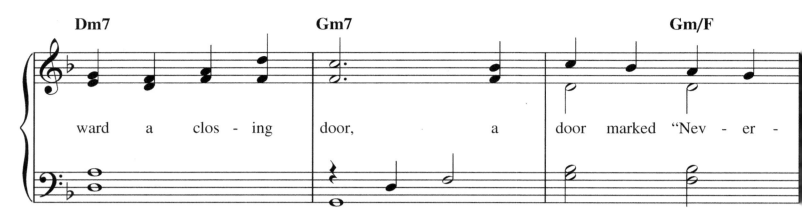

Dm7 · Gm7 · Gm/F

ward a clos - ing door, a door marked "Nev - er -

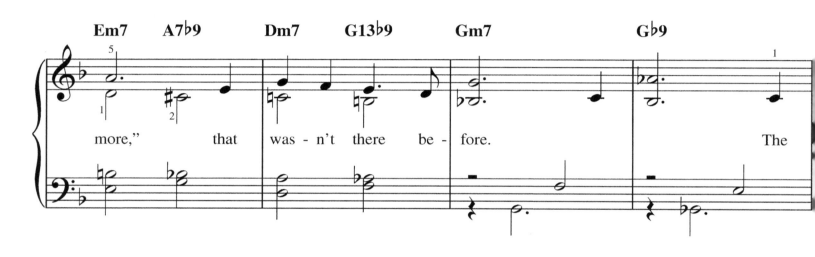

Em7 · A7♭9 · Dm7 · G13♭9 · Gm7 · G♭9

more," that was - n't there be - fore. The

F · F/E · F/E♭ · D7♯5 · D7♭5 · D7

lone - ly night dis - clos - es just a

Gm7 · B♭m6

pass - ing breeze filled with mem - o - ries

CRAZY WORLD
from VICTOR/VICTORIA

Lyrics by LESLIE BRICUSSE
Music by HENRY MANCINI

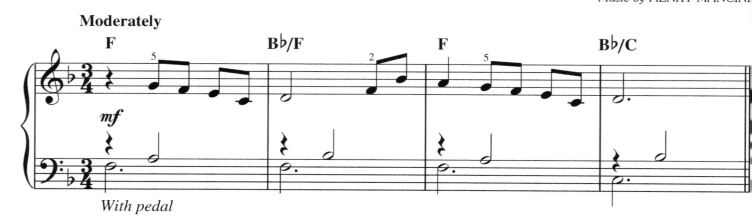

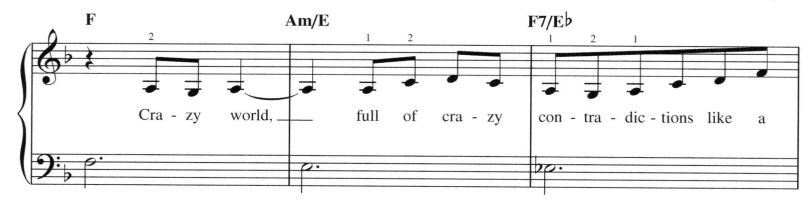

Cra - zy world, ___ full of cra - zy con - tra - dic - tions like a

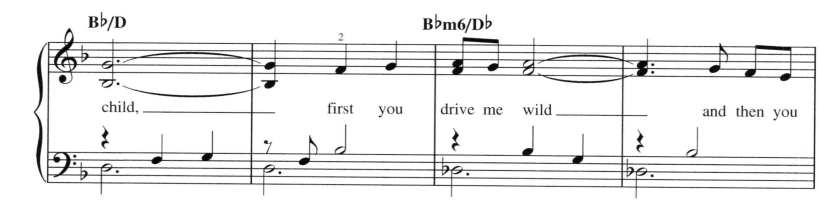

child, ___ first you drive me wild ___ and then you

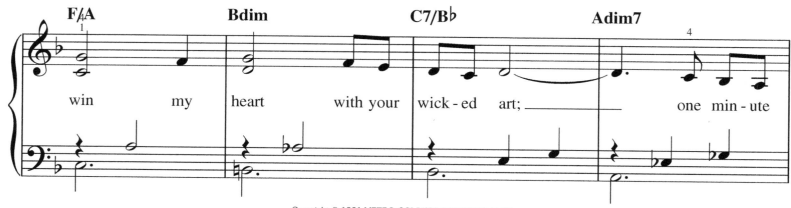

win my heart with your wick - ed art; ___ one min - ute

18

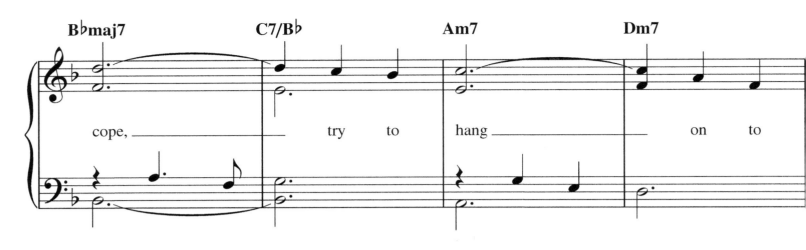

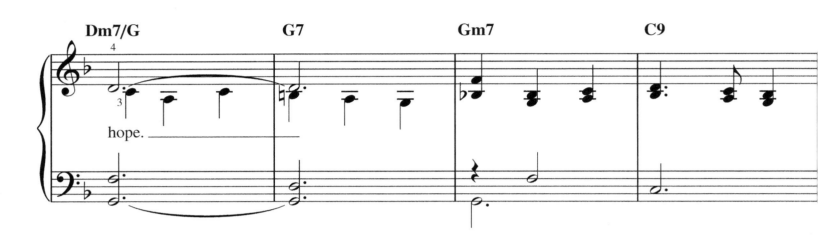

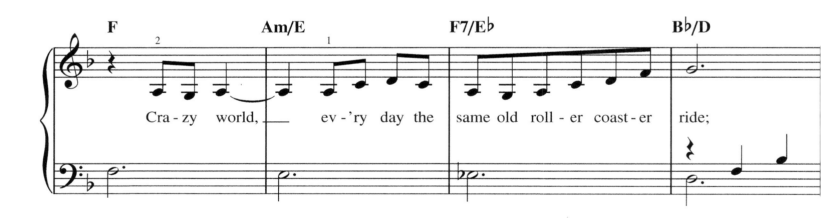

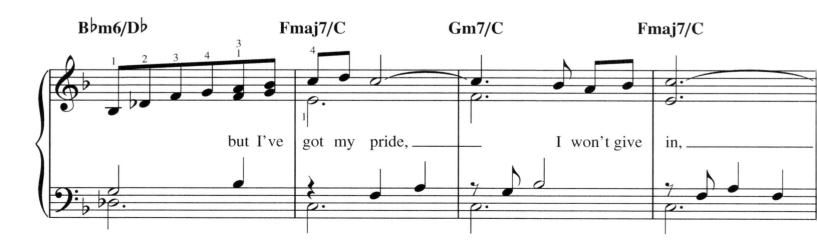

THE DANCING CAT

By HENRY MANCINI

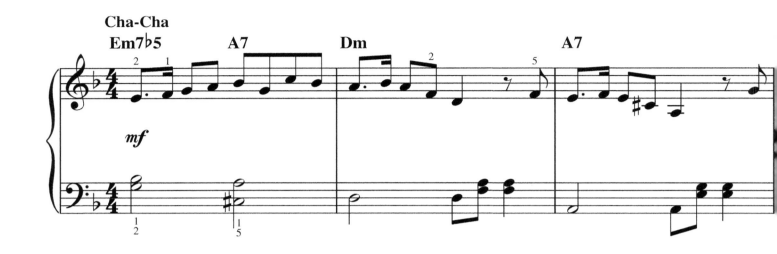

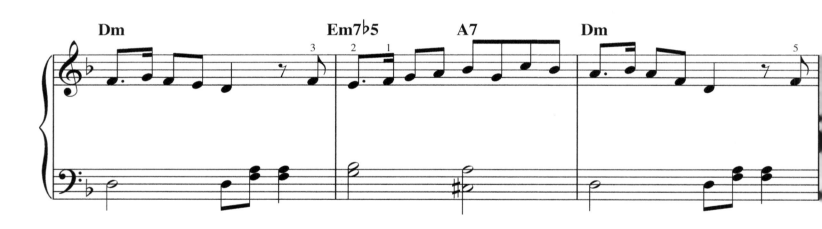

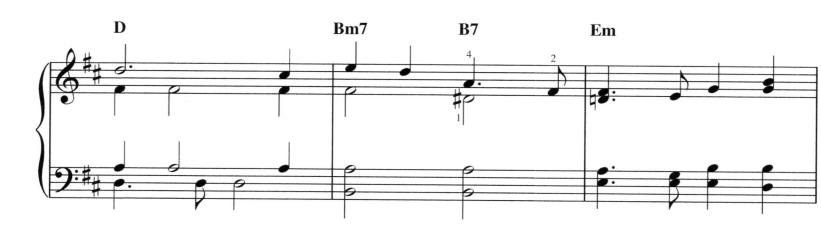

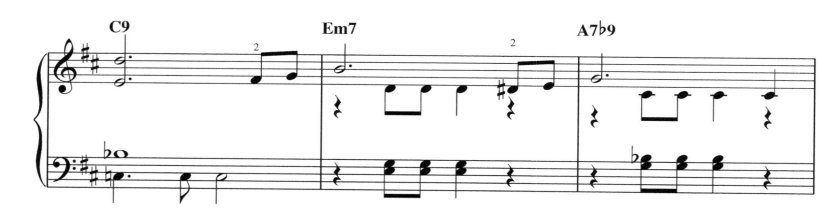

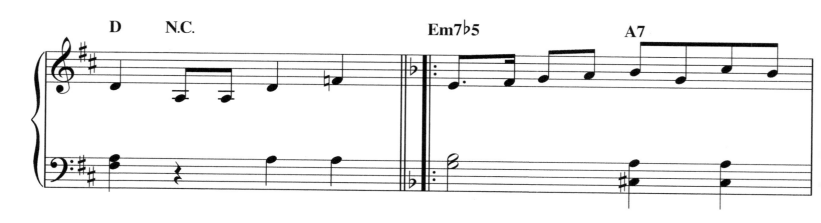

DARLING LILI

Words by JOHNNY MERCER
Music by HENRY MANCINI

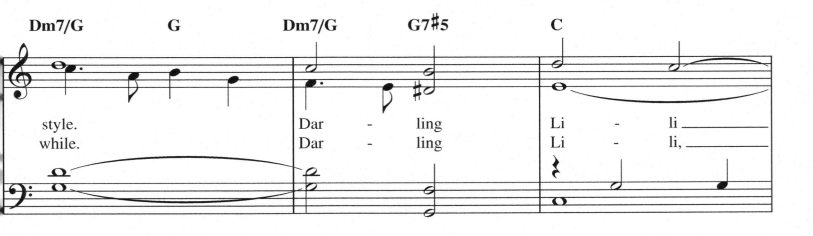

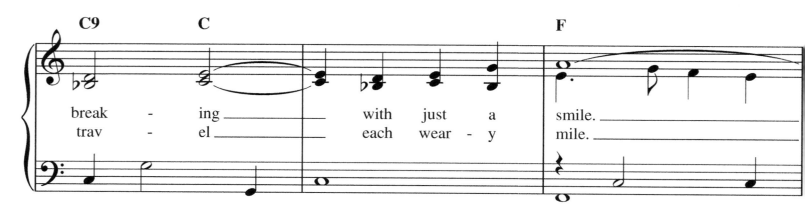

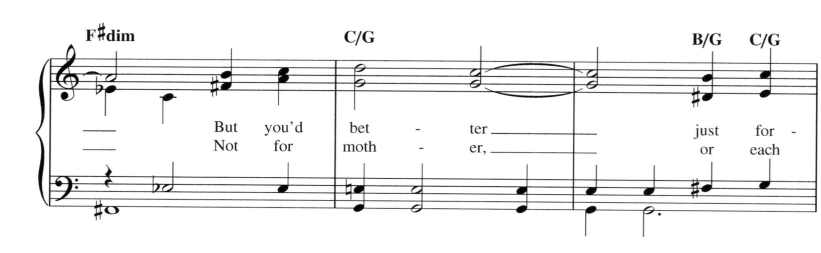

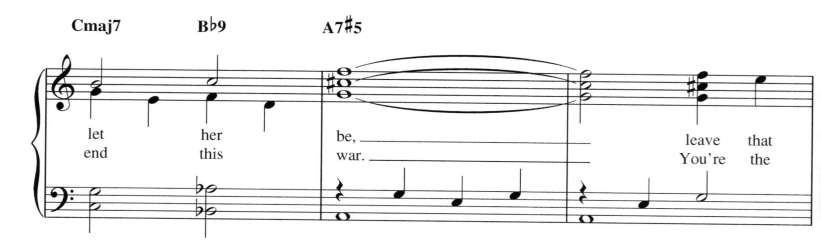

DEAR HEART
from DEAR HEART

Music by HENRY MANCINI
Words by JAY LIVINGSTON and RAY EVANS

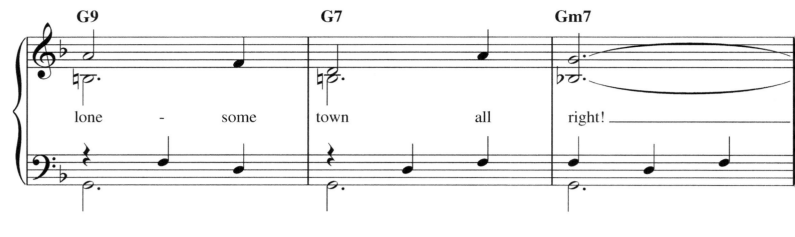

G9 **G7** **Gm7**

lone - some town all right! _____

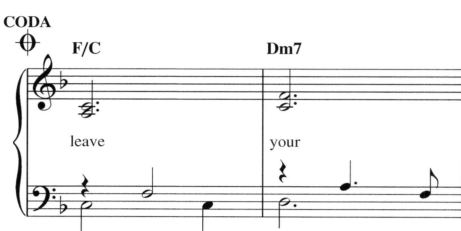

C7 **D.S. al Coda** **CODA** **F/C** **Dm7**
C7#5♭9

___ But leave your

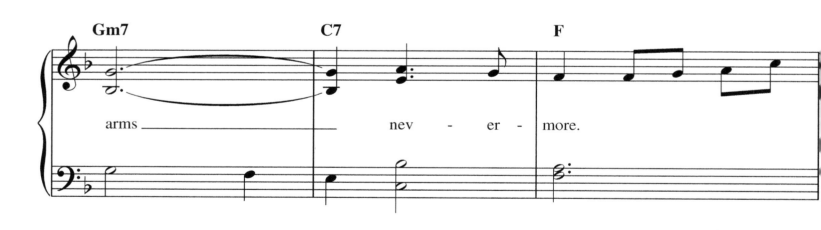

Gm7 **C7** **F**

arms _____ nev - er - more.

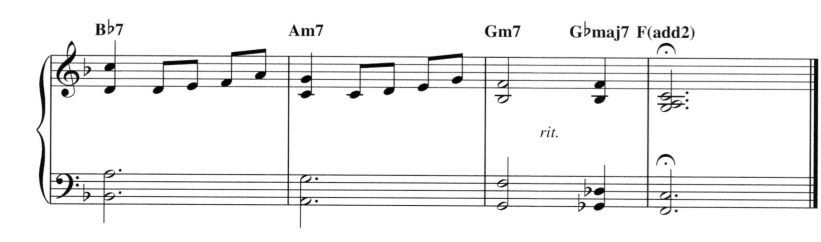

B♭7 **Am7** **Gm7** **G♭maj7 F(add2)**

rit.

DREAMSVILLE

Lyrics by JAY LIVINGSTON and RAY EVANS
Music by HENRY MANCINI

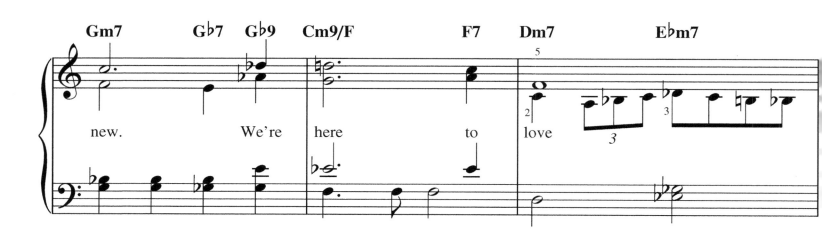

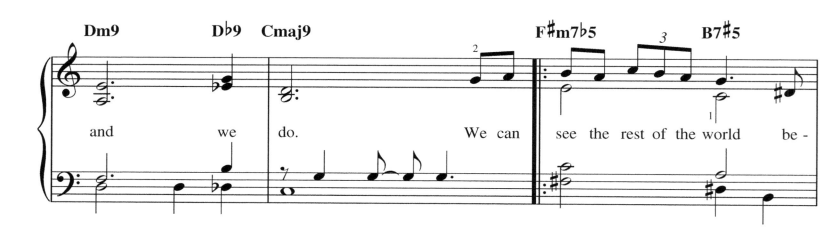

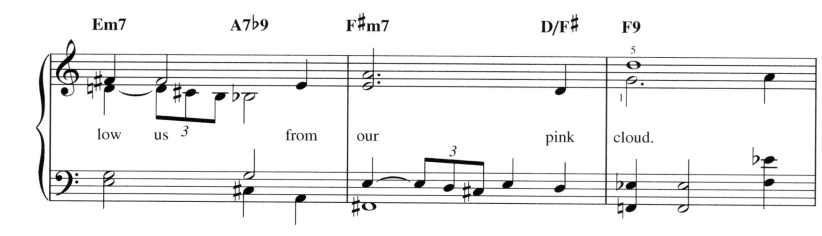

IN THE ARMS OF LOVE

Words by RAY EVANS and JAY LIVINGSTON
Music by HENRY MANCINI

hours go by, I'd show you why we've wait - ed for

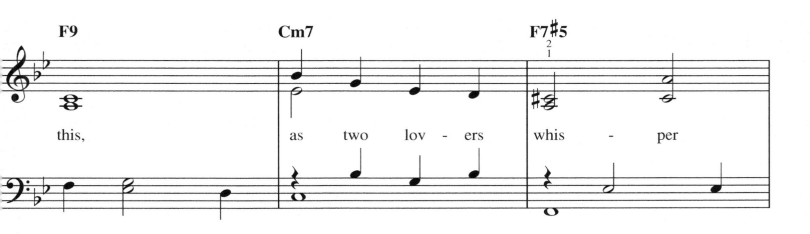

this, as two lov - ers whis - per

low. _____ If I could feel that

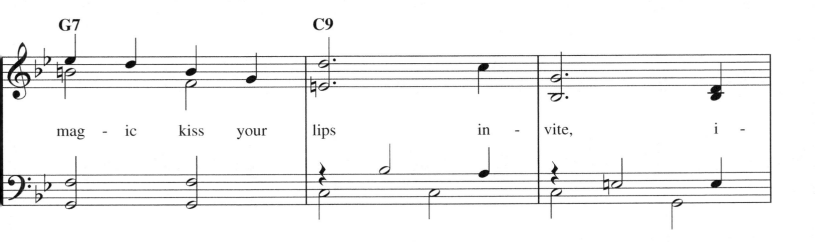

mag - ic kiss your lips in - vite, i -

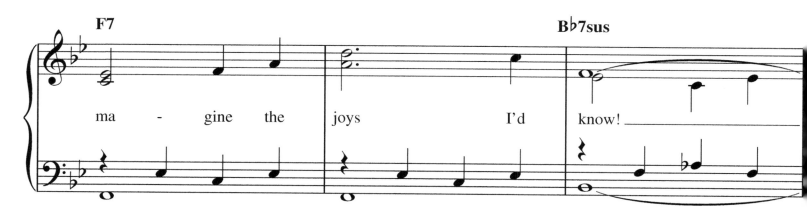

ma - gine the joys I'd know! _____

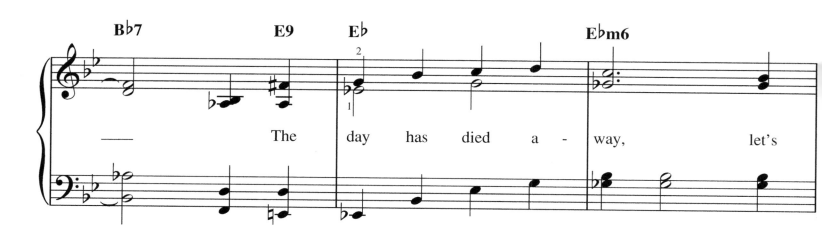

_____ The day has died a - way, let's

find a hide - a - way, and share the prom - ise

of a new to - mor - row,

INSPECTOR CLOUSEAU THEME

By HENRY MANCINI

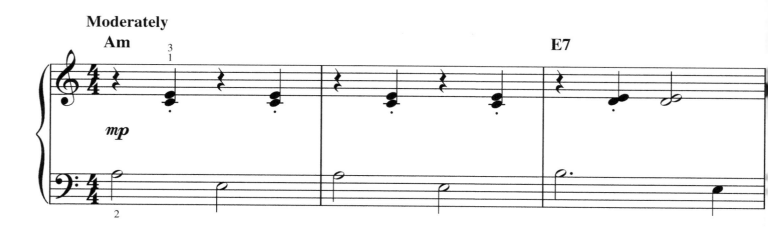

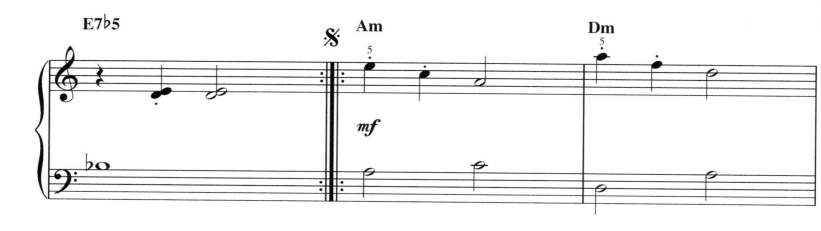

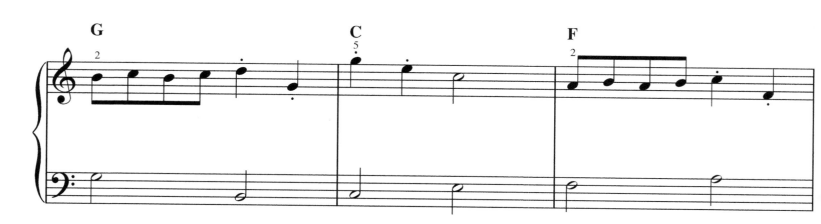

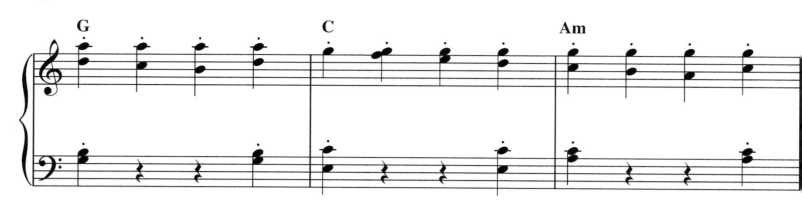

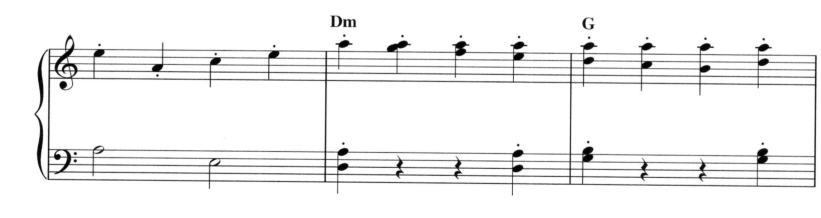

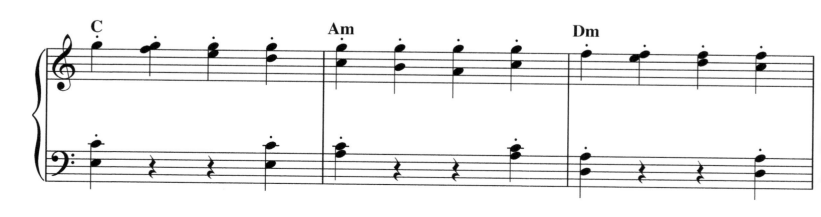

LIFE IN A LOOKING GLASS

Lyrics by LESLIE BRICUSSE
Music by HENRY MANCINI

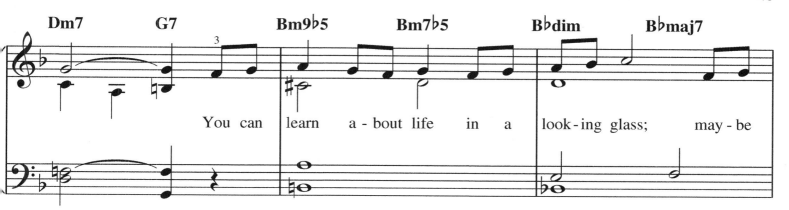

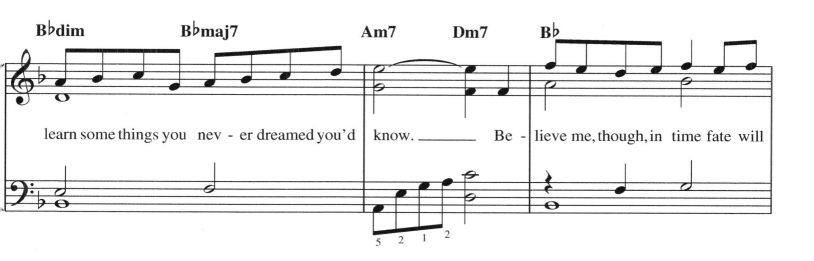

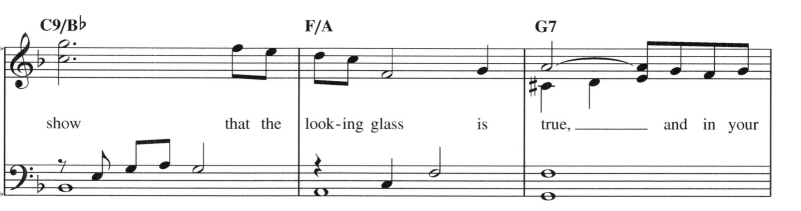

see. And you'll know who you are, and be glad you're

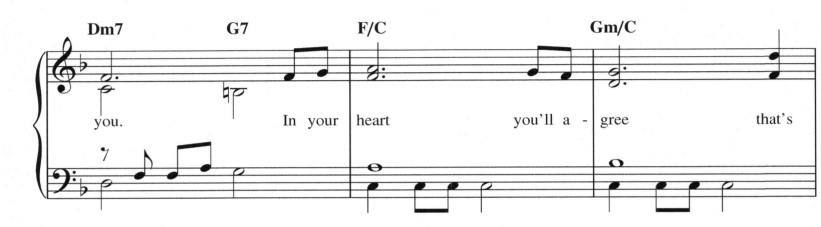

you. In your heart you'll a-gree that's

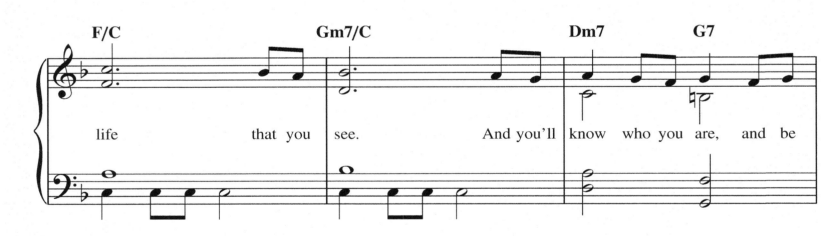

life that you see. And you'll know who you are, and be

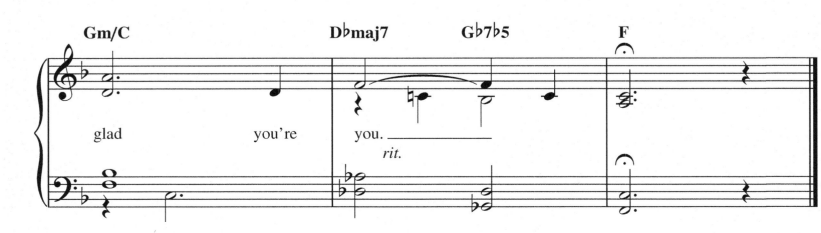

glad you're you. _____

rit.

MR. LUCKY

Lyrics by JAY LIVINGSTON and RAY EVANS
Music by HENRY MANCINI

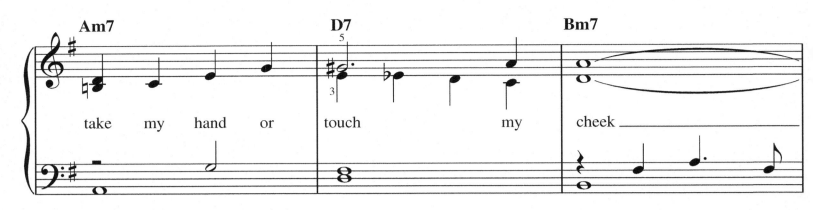

take my hand or touch my cheek ____

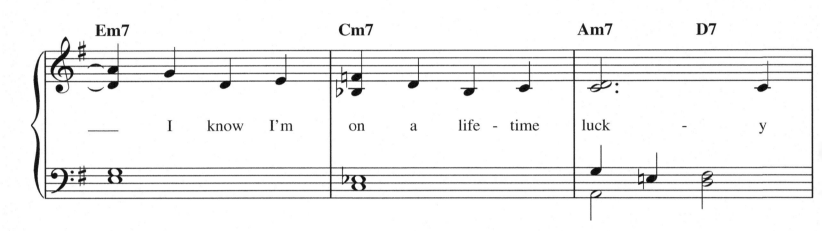

____ I know I'm on a life - time luck - y

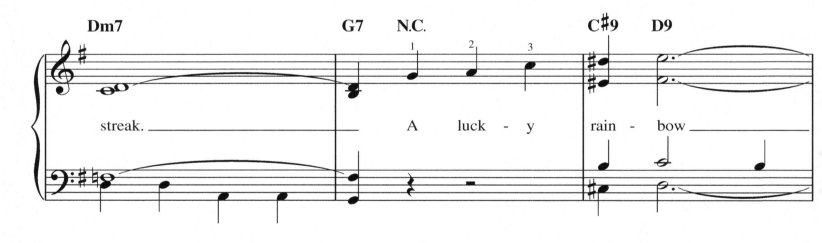

streak. ____ A luck - y rain - bow ____

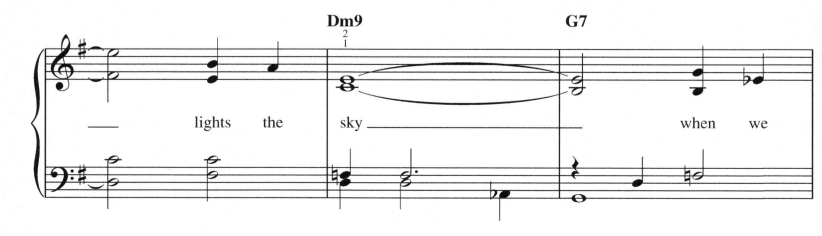

____ lights the sky ____ when we

MOMENT TO MOMENT

By HENRY MANCINI

see you,   to   touch you,   to i - ma - gine this   will

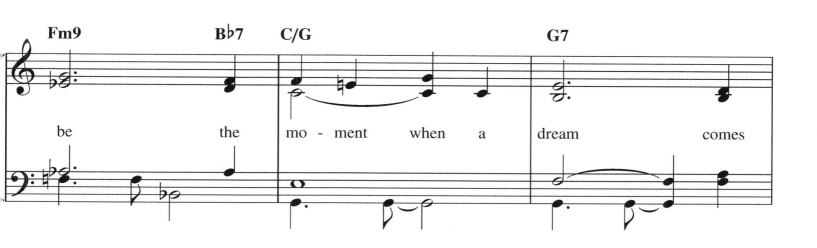

be   the   mo - ment   when   a   dream   comes

true. _____   Just an or - di - nar - y   day   be -

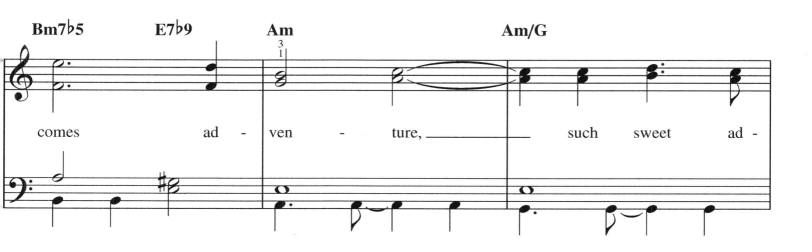

comes   ad - ven - ture, _____   such   sweet   ad -

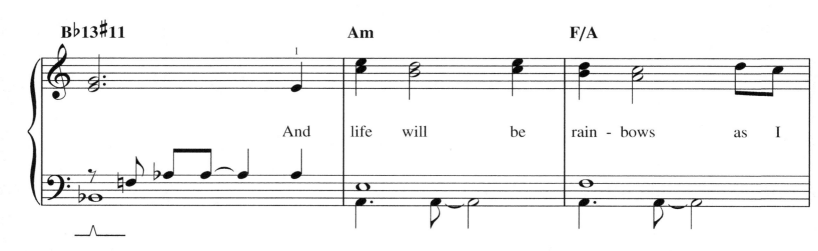

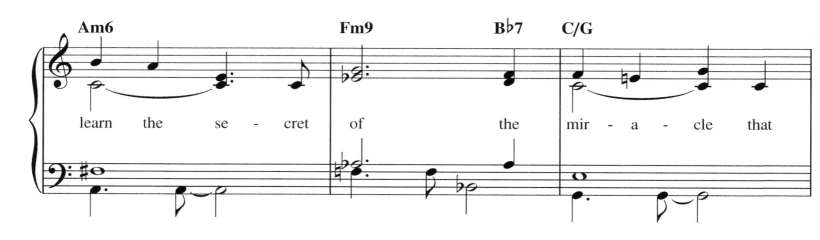

MOON RIVER

from the Paramount Picture BREAKFAST AT TIFFANY'S

Words by JOHNNY MERCER
Music by HENRY MANCINI

Slowly and expressively

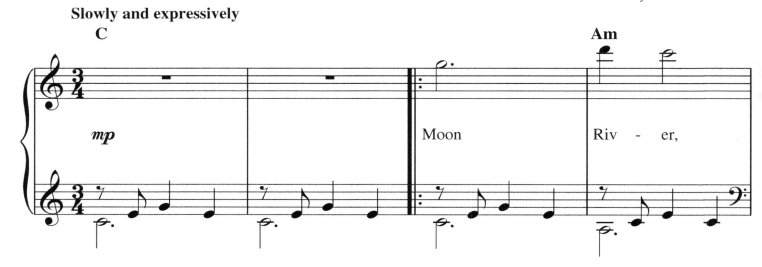

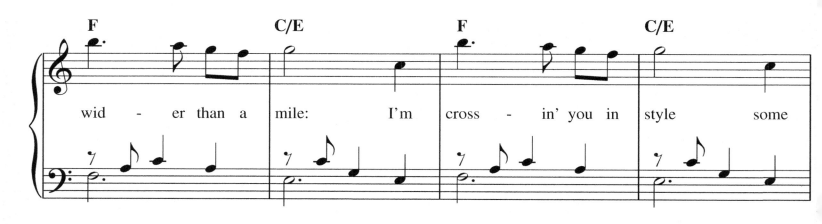

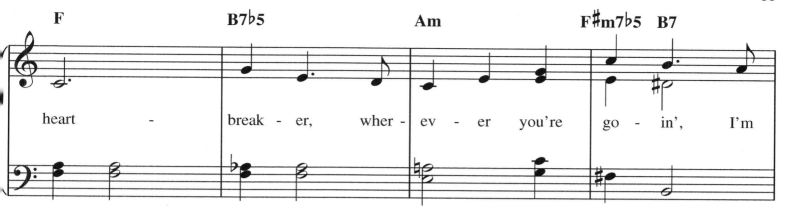

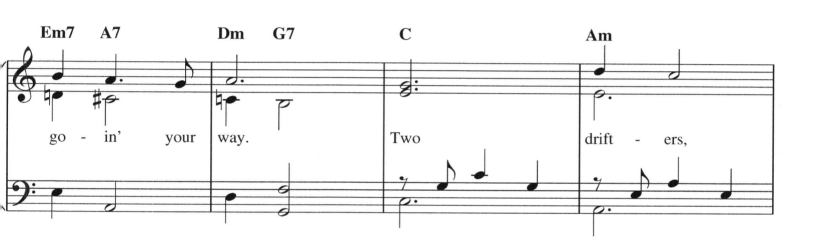

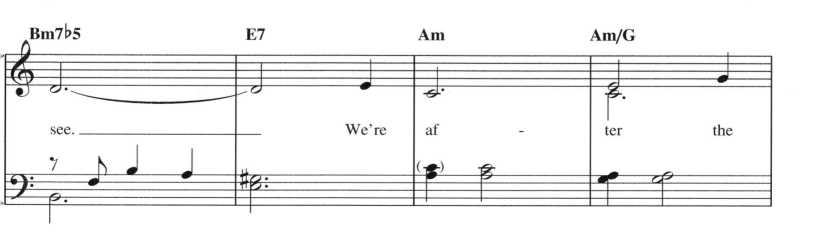

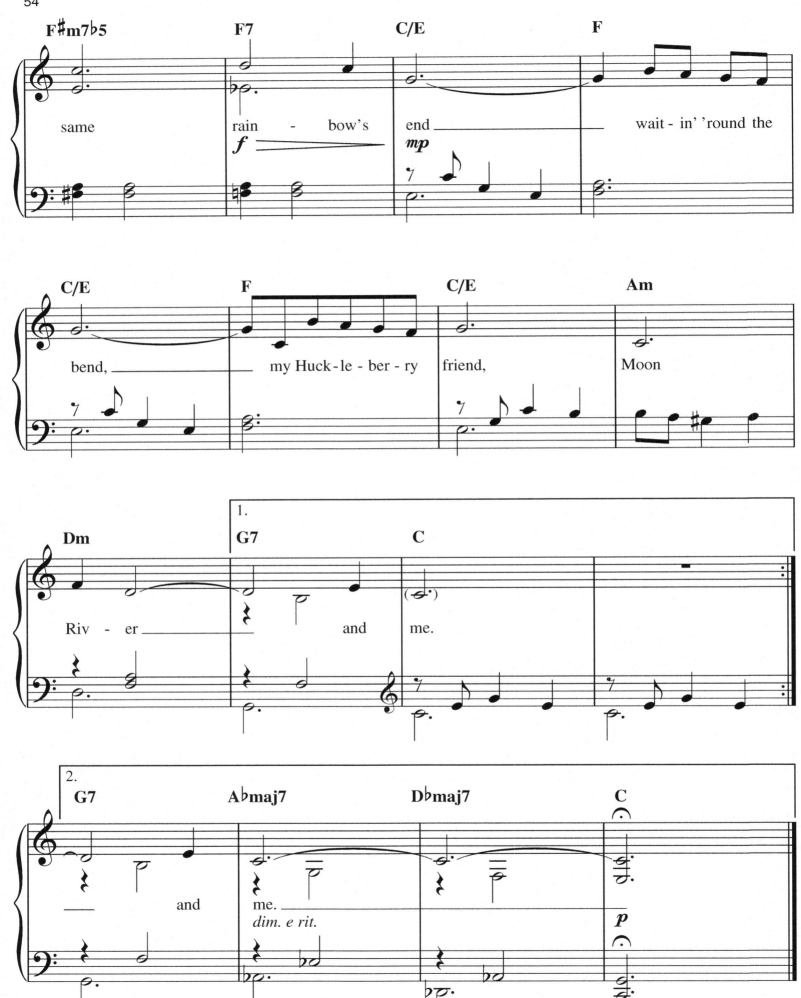

THE PINK PANTHER

from THE PINK PANTHER

By HENRY MANCINI

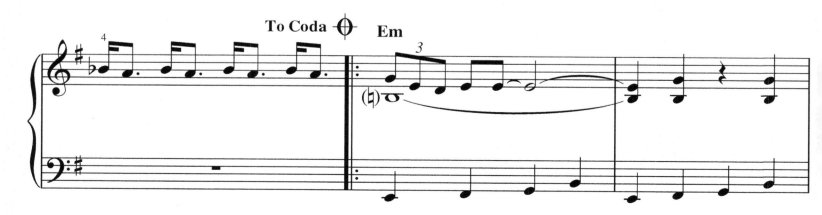

PETER GUNN
Theme Song from the Television Series

By HENRY MANCINI

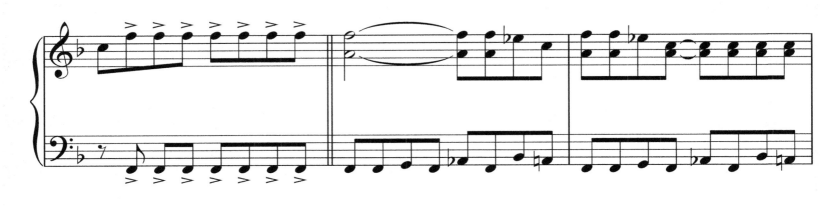

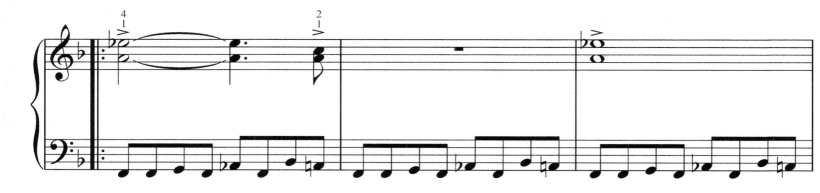

A SHOT IN THE DARK

from the Motion Picture A SHOT IN THE DARK

Words by LESLIE BRICUSSE
Music by HENRY MANCINI

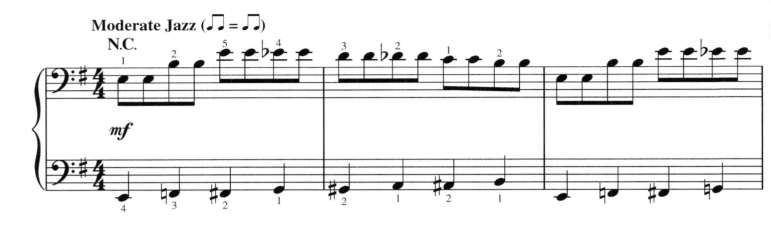

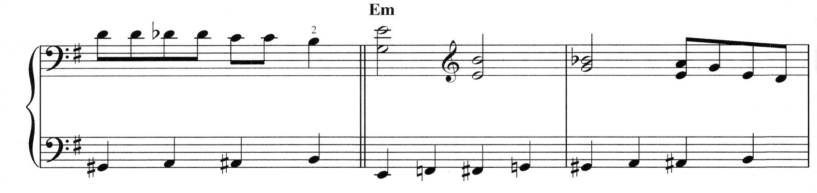

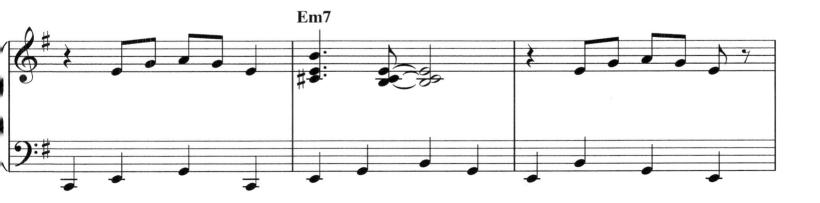

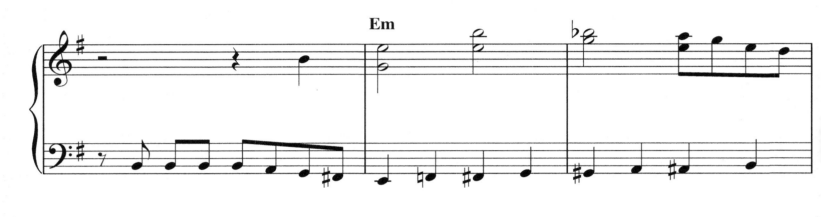

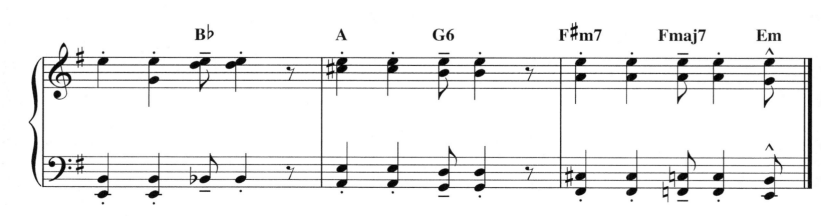

THE SWEETHEART TREE

from THE GREAT RACE

Words by JOHNNY MERCER
Music by HENRY MANCINI

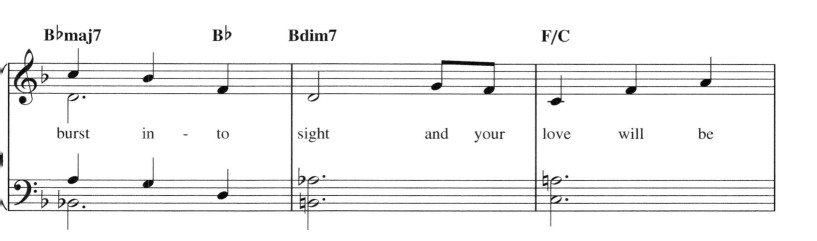

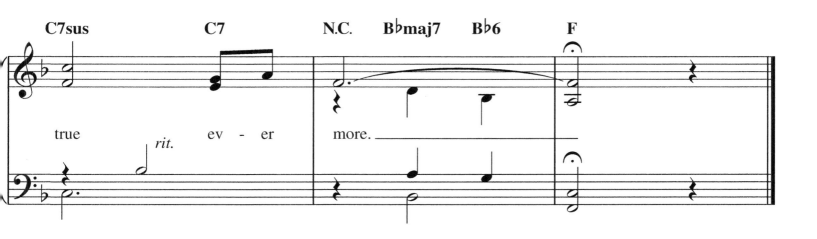

THE THORN BIRDS
(Main Theme)

By HENRY MANCINI

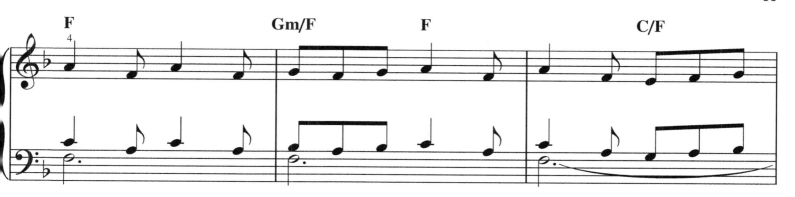

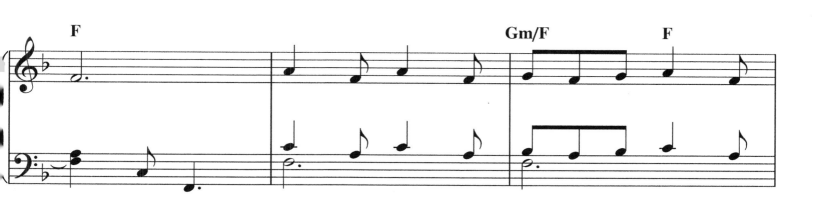

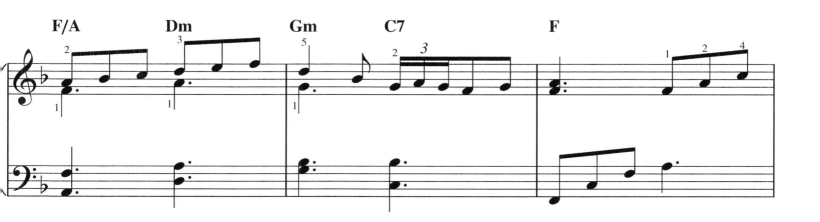

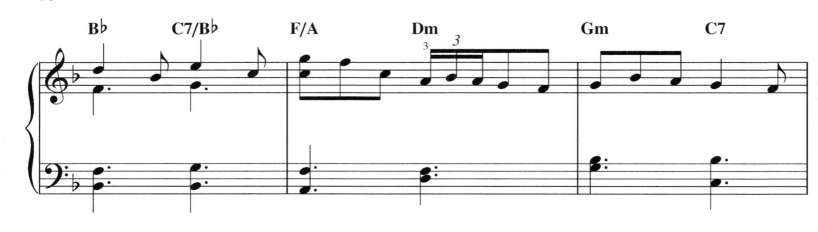

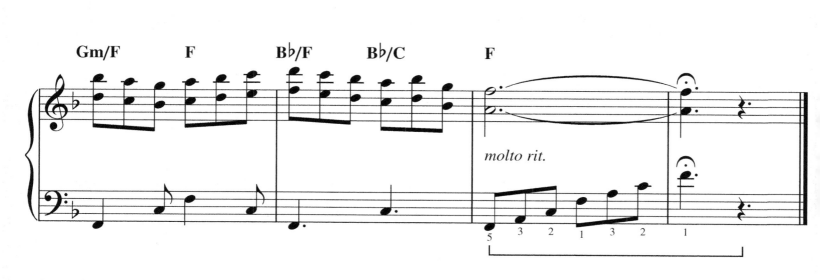

TWO FOR THE ROAD

Music by HENRY MANCINI
Words by LESLIE BRICUSSE

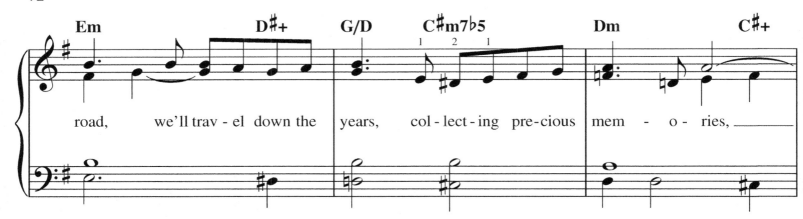

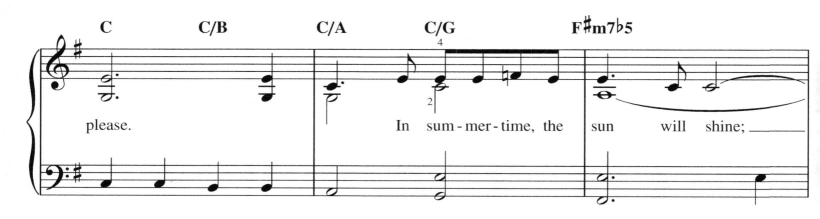

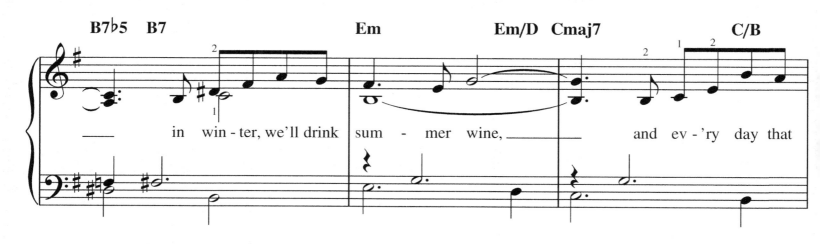

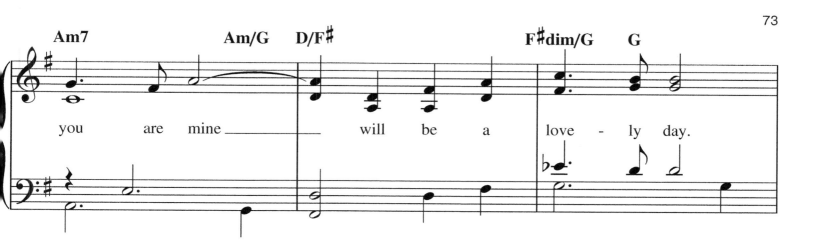

you are mine _____ will be a love - ly day.

As long as love still wears a smile, I

know that we'll be two for the road, and that's a long, long

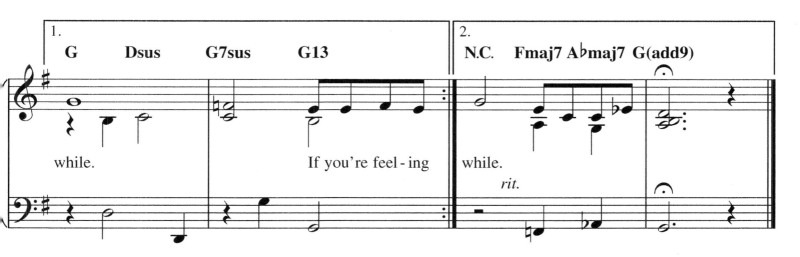

while. If you're feel-ing while.

rit.

WHISTLING AWAY THE DARK

Words by JOHNNY MERCER
Music by HENRY MANCINI

park.　　　　　　　To　keep　their　spir - it　soar -

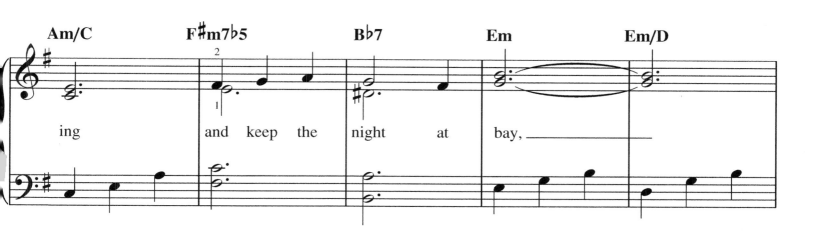

ing　　　　and　keep　the　night　at　bay, _____

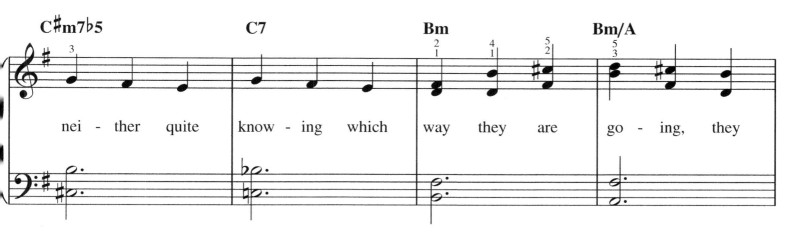

nei - ther　quite　know - ing　which　way　they　are　go - ing,　they

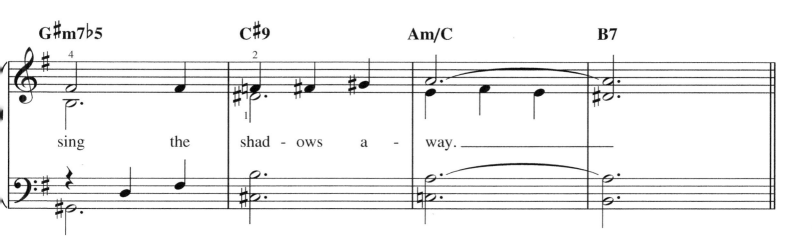

sing　　　the　shad - ows　a - way. _____

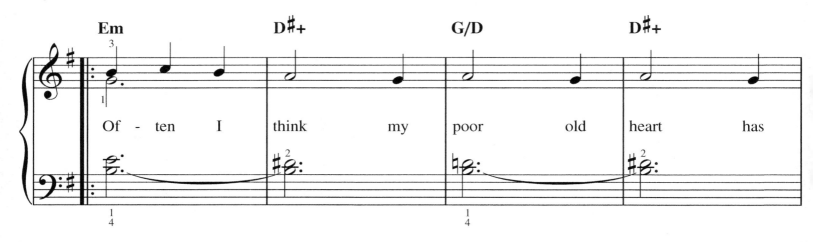

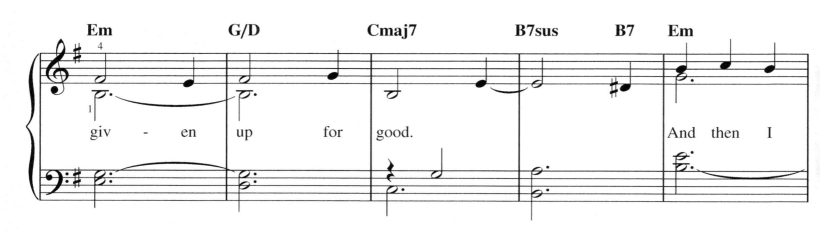

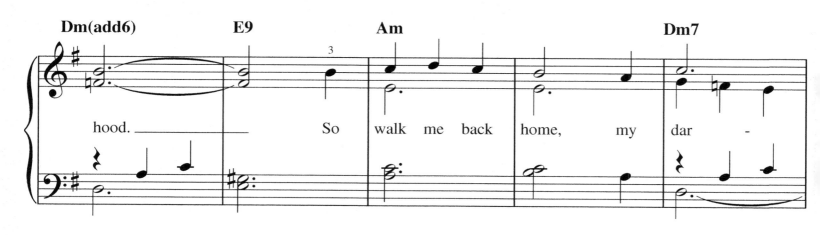

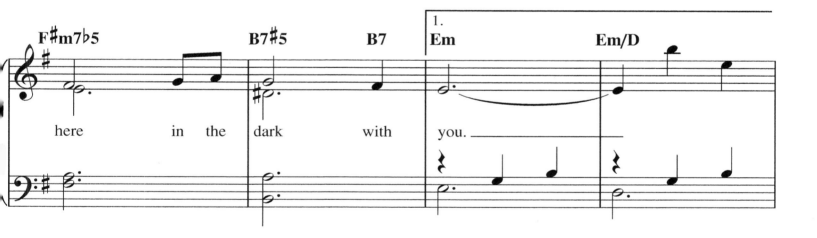